German Americans

SPIRIT
of America®

German AMERICANS

By C. Ann Fitterer

The Child's World®
Chanhassen, Minnesota

7

German AMERICANS

Published in the United States of America by The Child's World®
PO Box 326 • Chanhassen, MN 55317-0326 • 800-599-READ • www.childsworld.com

Acknowledgments

The Child's World®: Mary Berendes, Publishing Director

Editorial Directions, Inc.: E. Russell Primm, Emily Dolbear, Sarah E. De Capua, and Lucia Raatma, Editors; Linda S. Koutris, Photo Selector; Image Select International, Photo Research; Red Line Editorial and Pam Rosenberg, Fact Research; Tim Griffin/IndexServ, Indexer; Chad Rubel, Proofreader

Photos

Cover/frontispiece: A German-American farm family from Lincoln County, Nebraska, in 1938

Cover photographs ©: Library of Congress; Adam Woolfitt/Corbis

Interior photographs ©: Corbis, 6, 7 top; AKG-images, Berlin, 7 bottom, Ann Ronan Picture Library, 8; Getty Images, 9; Corbis, 10; Getty Images, 11; Corbis, 12; AKG-images, Berlin, 13 top; Ann Ronan Picture Library, 13 bottom; Getty Images, 15; Corbis, 16, 17; AKG-images, Berlin, 18, 19 left; Corbis, 19 right, 20; TRIP/J. Greenberg, 21; Corbis, 22, 23, 24, 25 top; Getty Images, 25 bottom; TRIP/H. Rogers, 26 top; Getty Images, 26 bottom; Corbis, 27; Ann Ronan Picture Library, 29 top; TRIP/S. Grant, 29 bottom.

Library of Congress Cataloging-in-Publication Data

Fitterer, C. Ann.
German Americans / by C. Ann Fitterer.
   p. cm.
Includes index.
Summary: Brief introduction to German Americans, their reasons for immigrating to the United States, customs and traditions, and their impact on American society.
ISBN 1-56766-151-3 (lib. bd. : alk. paper)
1. German Americans--Juvenile literature. 2. Immigrants—United States—Juvenile literature. [1. German Americans.] I. Title.
E184.G3 F58 2003
305.831073—dc21
                                   2001007389

16   19   26

Contents

Chapter ONE

The First German Immigrants

THE PEOPLE OF THE UNITED STATES CAN TRACE their **heritage** to almost every other country in the world. A large group of Americans trace their **ancestors** to **immigrants** who came from German-speaking countries. German Americans are not necessarily people whose ancestors came only from the country of Germany. When the first German-speaking people emigrated to America, there was no single country known as Germany. Instead, there were many German-speaking kingdoms.

Levenworth, Washington, is just one of the many American towns with a German atmosphere.

German settlements were spread over a large area of Europe. All these people had a common language, however. They all spoke German.

German immigrants have been coming to America for more than 300 years. German-speaking immigrants settled the first non-English town in America. In 1683, they settled in an area that is now part of the city of Philadelphia, Pennsylvania. The Germans built a town and named it Germantown. The layout of the town and the style of the houses looked just like those in Germany.

Old City Hall in Germantown, Pennsylvania

Many Germans came to America with hopes of religious freedom.

At that time in Europe, many wars were being fought. The fighting was among several religious groups. The leading church would not allow people to follow other religions. The settlers who built

Germantown came to America to escape the fighting. Also, in America, they were able to choose the religion they wished to follow.

Many German people followed this first group of immigrants. Most of them settled around Philadelphia. Thousands of Germans came to America over the next 70 years. Almost three-fourths of them settled in the **colonies** of New York, New Jersey, and Pennsylvania.

In the early 1800s, more than 5 million Germans settled in the Midwestern states of Missouri, Illinois, Indiana, Wisconsin, Michigan, and Minnesota. Many settled in Texas. These German immigrants were different from the immigrants of the 1600s and 1700s. They were not seeking religious freedom. But they hoped to find a more prosperous life. In Germany, people were suffering

Conestoga wagons carried thousands of settlers into the American plains.

8

from lack of food, poor **harvests** on their farms, not enough land to start new farms, and a shortage of jobs. America offered opportunities to get jobs, begin successful farms, and enjoy plenty of food.

In the 1880s, another large group of Germans came

Germans endured long, crowded sea voyages on their way to the United States.

to America. By this time, the rich farmland of the Midwest was mostly taken, so these immigrants settled in Kansas, Nebraska, North Dakota, and South Dakota. That land had been considered the "dry desert" of America. But it was similar to the land these new immigrants had farmed in Europe, and they built successful farms.

Another group of German immigrants came to America in the 1900s. These people came for neither religious freedom, nor jobs, nor food. They left their home countries because of their politics and government. These immigrants were not farmers, as the earlier Germans were. They were well-educated people with money and good jobs. They settled in many major American cities.

Germans have been coming to America for many reasons over the past 300 years. But, whatever the reason, these people made the long and difficult trip hoping for a better life in America than they could find in their homeland.

The site of New York City must have been exciting for German immigrants as they finished their journey across the Atlantic.

10

MOLLY PITCHER LIVED DURING THE 1700S. SHE WAS THE DAUGHTER of German immigrants. At birth, her name was Maria Ludwig, and her family lived near Trenton, New Jersey. She married a young barber, who later enlisted in the Continental army during the Revolutionary War (1775–1783).

Many of the soldiers' wives traveled with their husbands to the places where the army had sent them. Molly went with her

husband to Valley Forge, Pennsylvania. The wives helped by cooking, cleaning, washing, and mending the soldiers' clothes. On Sunday, June 28, 1778, Molly's husband fought in the Battle of Monmouth.

Molly carried water to the soldiers to help ease their thirst while they fought. During the battle, her husband was wounded and could not fire his cannon. Molly jumped into his position and fired his cannon alongside the rest of the soldiers until the battle ended.

Chapter Two

Living in a New Country

A German-American farm in Wisconsin

LIFE IN AMERICA FOR GERMAN IMMIGRANTS was varied. Because of the enormous number of German immigrants, it is almost impossible to describe their experiences as being similar.

Some Germans settled on farms in rural areas. They often lived in clusters, so they were able to continue many of the **traditions** they enjoyed in their homeland. They continued to speak German, and their children were taught in German at school. These farmers were well respected for their skills in growing excellent crops, raising quality animals, and having well-kept gardens and homesteads.

Some areas of the United States even advertised in Germany, trying to get these skilled farmers to settle and produce successful crops in areas considered poor for farming. Louisiana was one state that did this.

The Southern tradition of slavery was viewed as unjust by most German Americans.

Few Germans settled in the South. The land there was not as fertile as land in other parts of the country. In addition, most German settlers did not like the Southern practice of slavery. They did not believe that slavery was just.

Most German immigrants, especially those who arrived during and after the 1880s, settled in large cities. Three popular cities for Germans to live in at that time were Cincinnati, Ohio; St. Louis, Missouri; and Chicago, Illinois. Often, there were German neighborhoods in these cities. Many German people found work in the brewing industry. There, German immigrants worked in the production of beer and other beverages. Other Germans got jobs in the tanning industry where animal hides were made into leather. Milling, or turning wheat into usable flour, and construction jobs were also popular with German immigrants.

Some German Americans found work in breweries in the Midwest.

▶ The German immigrants who arrived in America in the 1700s brought with them the tradition of building houses made of logs. They taught others how to notch the ends of the logs, place them together, and fill the cracks with a type of cement.

German immigrants struggled to feel comfortable in their new country. Many of the other settlers were British or Irish. They spoke English. The Germans did not. This made them stand out, and it kept them separated from other newcomers. It was also difficult to know the **customs** of their new land. Many Germans tried to continue all their German customs, while at the same time trying to learn the new ones of America. This was hard. Many Americans were unkind to the Germans. Sometimes German immigrants even experienced violent attacks.

Some German beliefs and traditions made many Americans dislike them even more. Many German Americans spoke out against slavery before the American Civil War (1861–1865). However, they criticized the Southern states that had **seceded** from the **Union**. They were strong supporters of the United States and believed that all the states should work together. These sentiments angered Southerners, who believed the South should be a separate country. The Germans' love of dancing, music, and celebrations also offended some Americans. They resented the way the Germans bowled, danced, and drank beer on the Sabbath Day, or Sunday.

During the 1900s, life for German Americans was especially difficult because Germany had been the enemy of the United States in both World War I (1914–1918) and World War II (1939–1945). There were many anti-German organizations in the United States, and Americans were suspicious of people who were connected with Germany in any way.

As difficult as it was for German Americans to feel they belonged in their new country, their actions reflected their courage and their commitment to remain in America and build a bright future. They started schools and formed community and drama groups. They were known for organizing clubs that supported people in need. They started Turnvereine groups—athletic clubs that originated in Germany. Throughout all this, the German Americans also found ways to make music a part of their everyday lives. It was this music, perhaps, that gave the German Americans much of the strength they needed to continue making new lives in America.

Nazi troops during World War II, a trying time for German Americans

WHEN IMMIGRANTS FIRST LANDED IN AMERICA, OFFICIALS met them as they came off their ship. As more and more immigrants came to America, a larger immigration center was clearly needed. It was built in New York Harbor on a small piece of land known as Ellis Island.

Ellis Island opened in 1892. Over the next 30 years, more than 12 million immigrants passed through the immigration center there (below).

Only the poorest passengers on a ship had to go through Ellis Island though. People with more expensive tickets met with officials while they were still onboard the ship.

When immigrants landed at Ellis Island, they went inside the

building. After leaving their baggage, they were examined by doctors and immigration officials. The doctors and officials checked to make sure the immigrants had no diseases and that they were in good mental health. If a doctor or an official thought someone was not healthy, that person was sent back to his or her homeland. Immigrants did their best to look and act healthy so that they could stay in America.

Ellis Island closed in 1954. By then, it was in run-down condition because it had been neglected for many years. However, Ellis Island was restored in 1990 and opened as an immigration museum (above). It draws millions of visitors every year.

Chapter THREE

Famous German Americans

Werner von Braun played a key role in the U.S. space program

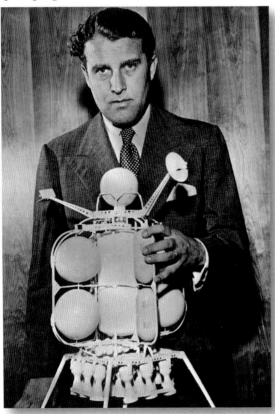

MILLIONS OF AMERICANS TODAY ARE THE descendants of German-speaking immigrants. Because they have been part of America for more than 300 years, German Americans have had a longer period than other immigrant groups to become a part of American **culture**.

Americans of German descent live in every part of the United States. They have become important members of U.S. society and many are now famous.

America is known throughout the world for its space program. After World War II (1939–1945), an engineer named Werner von

Two famous German Americans, Albert Einstein (left) and John Augustus Roebling (right)

Braun and a team of rocket scientists came to the United States from Germany. They are responsible for putting the first American **satellite** into orbit in 1958. Later, they developed the launch vehicle for the Apollo space program.

One of America's most famous writers and experts in American English was a German American named Henry Mencken. Mencken lived during the first half of the 20th century. Some of the most significant events in science were achieved by German Americans such as Albert Einstein. Architects, such as Ludwig

Interesting Fact

In 1990, the United States had 522,252 farmers of German descent. That was almost three times as many as those of English descent and more than three times the number of farmers of Scandinavian descent.

19

Mies van der Rohe, who designed American skyscrapers, trace their roots to Germany. Another German architect, John Augustus Roebling, invented the method of building **suspension bridges**. He designed, and his son built, New York City's Brooklyn Bridge, which opened in 1883. Today, the Brooklyn Bridge is one of the city's most recognizable landmarks.

Early German Americans were not politically active. However, that is not the case in modern America. Dwight D. Eisenhower, the 34th president of the United States, was descended from German and Swiss immigrants. He served from 1953 to 1961.

As political relations with Germany have

Dwight D. Eisenhower, 34th president of the United States

become more friendly in the past 50 years, anti-German organizations and feelings are no longer a problem. German communities continue to hold their festivals with pride. Their dancing and singing attracts people from many ethnic groups.

Americans of all backgrounds enjoy celebrating the German festival of Octoberfest.

Today, German Americans take pride in their German ancestry, but they are equally proud to be Americans. They have blended into American society. They hold jobs in every area of business, education, and government.

IN THE EARLY 1900S, A POLITICAL GROUP CALLED THE NAZIS were controlling Germany and surrounding countries. Life was dangerous for anyone who did not agree with the Nazis.

One such group who did not follow the ways of the Nazis was the von Trapp family (below) in Austria. Their story became the famous book, film, and play called *The Sound of Music*. This is the story of how Maria von Trapp left the convent to take care of the von Trapp children, fell in love with their father, the Baron von Trapp, and married him.

In 1938, the von Trapp family did, indeed, escape the Nazi government by hiking across the Swiss Alps to safety in Italy. They had

nothing but the clothes they were wearing and some hiking packs on their backs. They had no money and were not citizens. One of their hobbies was singing. They decided to sing together, performing for money. They were very good, and soon they were touring all over Europe, performing for large audiences. In 1939, they were performing in the United States and visited the town of Stowe, Vermont (above). They ended up settling there and becoming United States citizens. Today, their home, which they used as a lodge for music camps, is still a lodge open for visitors. It is called the Trapp Family Lodge and is run by the Baron and Maria's youngest son, Johannes.

Chapter FOUR

German-American Contributions

AMERICAN CULTURE HAS BEEN GREATLY influenced by German immigrants. Not only have individual people had a significant impact with inventions and achievements, but many things we use in everyday life also came from the German culture.

Many American foods have German origins, for example. Hamburgers, frankfurters (or hot dogs), sausages, sauerkraut, and potato salad are some of the German foods that are a regular part of the American diet. Ketchup, found in most American homes and restaurants, was produced by German-American H. J. Heinz.

Hamburgers and sausages are some of the German foods that have become part of American life.

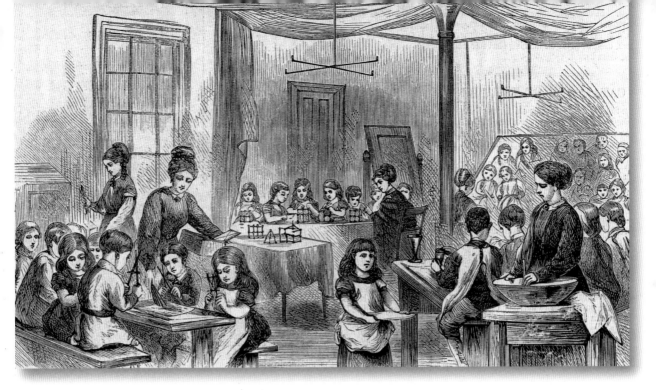

American schools have also been influenced by Germans. Kindergarten was common in Germany, but had never been heard of among English-speaking Americans. The first kindergarten in the United States was started by two German women. Caroline Louisa Frankenberg and Margarethe Meyer Schurz started their kindergarten programs in America in the mid-1800s. By 1880, there were 400 kindergartens in 30 states. Today, kindergarten is a

German contributions to education include kindergarten (above) and the work of Dr. Seuss (below).

25

Denim blue jeans were invented by Levi Strauss, a German American.

German Americans have provided improvements to U.S. farming and food production.

regular part of every young American's life. Almost every kindergartener today has heard the stories written by the famous Dr. Seuss, a German American whose real name was Theodor Seuss Geisel.

The clothing industry was greatly impacted by a man named Levi Strauss. He began manufacturing a type of men's pants made from a strong material called denim. The pants were styled to meet the needs of workingmen. Today we call these pants "jeans." His company still manufactures the jeans we know as Levi's.

People of German descent have influenced agriculture for hundreds of years. However, many modern ways of raising crops and live-

stock and managing land are the result of German immigrants and their descendants. Largely because of them, the United States has become a world leader in food production.

The field of medicine has also been influenced by German immigrants. Pediatrics is the branch of medicine that specializes in preventing and treating diseases in children. Three hundred years ago, there was no such specialty. Children were treated the same way—and with the same medicines—as adults. In the 1800s, a German American named Abraham Jacobi changed that. Today's pediatricians give credit to him as the Father of Pediatrics.

Dr. Abraham Jacobi, the founder of American pediatrics

Many Americans believe the greatest gift from the German culture is their musical traditions. Music has always been important in German life. Everyone participated in some way: singing, playing an instrument, writing music, or directing a group of performers. When not performing, Germans took great pleasure in listening to music. Dancing often accompanied the music. Many famous American performers and composers are of German descent. One such composer was John Philip Sousa. He wrote songs that became famous for their upbeat patriotic

Composer and bandleader John Philip Sousa

The Christmas tree is a holiday symbol brought to the United States by German immigrants.

music. Americans today have parades during many celebrations. It is a rare parade that does not include a band playing a song written by Sousa.

Christmas is celebrated by many Americans. Two common symbols of an American Christmas are the Christmas tree and Santa Claus. The Christmas tree came from German immigrants who brought the tradition with them from Germany. The German word for Christmas tree is *Tannenbaum.* A popular Christmas carol is "Oh, Tannenbaum." The Germans also brought the tradition of Kris Kringle, or Santa Claus, as he is called in America.

The list of contributions to American culture from the German people and culture is seemingly endless. America's rich heritage has a strong tradition in the life of German immigrants, who brought their knowledge, skills, and customs to help shape America into what it is today.

1683 German immigrants establish the town of Germantown, Pennsylvania.

1683–1753 Thousands of German immigrants arrive in America, settling mostly in New York, New Jersey, and Pennsylvania.

1730 Baron Von Steuben is born in Germany. He later comes to the United States to lead colonial troops in the Revolutionary War and eventually becomes a U.S. citizen.

1775–1783 The American Revolutionary War is fought.

1800s More than 5 million Germans settle in the midwestern states of the United States.

1850 Two German women begin the first kindergarten program in the United States.

1861–1865 The American Civil War is fought.

1871 Wilhem I, formerly the King of Prussia, is the first ruler to hold the title of emperor over a united Germany.

1880s German immigrants settle on land in Kansas, Nebraska, North Dakota, and South Dakota.

1892 Ellis Island opens in New York Harbor.

1900s Political and governmental problems lead thousands of Germans to emigrate to the United States.

1914–1918 World War I is fought.

1933 Albert Einstein emigrates to the United States to escape the Nazi government. He accepts a teaching post at Princeton University and remains there for the rest of his life.

1939–1945 World War II is fought.

1953 German-American Dwight D. Eisenhower becomes the 34th president of the United States.

1954 Ellis Island closes.

1958 German immigrant Werner von Braun and his team of rocket scientists help put the first U.S. satellite into orbit.

1990 Ellis Island opens as an immigration museum.

Glossary

ancestors (AN-sess-turs)
Ancestors are family members who lived a long time ago. Many Americans' ancestors were immigrants.

colonies (KOL-uh-neez)
Colonies are territories controlled by faraway lands. Before America's independence, some areas of the United States were British colonies.

culture (KUHL-chur)
Culture is the way of life, ideas, customs, and traditions of a group of people. German Americans have greatly contributed to American culture.

customs (KUHSS-tuhms)
Customs are traditions in a culture. German immigrants often combined their old customs with new American ones.

harvests (HAR-vests)
A harvest is the gathering of crops. German immigrants in the 1800s hoped to have better harvests in America than they did in Germany.

heritage (HER-uh-tij)
Important traditions handed down for generation to generation make up each person's heritage. The people of the United States can trace their heritage to almost every country in the world.

immigrants (IM-ih-grents)
An immigrant is someone who comes from one country to live permanently in another country. Many Americans have ancestors who were immigrants.

satellite (SAT-eh-lite)
A satellite is a spacecraft sent into orbit around the Earth, the moon, or another heavenly body. A team of German scientists helped put the first American satellite into orbit.

seceded (sih-SEED-ed)
When a group secedes, it separates from a larger group. Many German Americans spoke out against the states that seceded from the Union before the Civil War.

**suspension bridges
(suh-SPEN-shuhn BRIJ-ez)**
A suspension bridge hangs from cables or chains strung from towers. New York City's Brooklyn Bridge is a suspension bridge.

traditions (truh-DISH-unz)
Traditions are the customs, ideas, and beliefs handed down for generations. German settlers in America brought traditions from Germany.

Union (YOON-yun)
The Union is another name for the United States of America. During the American Civil War, the northern states were called the Union.

Web Sites

Visit our homepage for lots of links about German Americans:
http://www.childsworld.com/links.html

Note to Parents, Teachers, and Librarians:
We routinely verify our Web links to make sure they're safe,
active sites—so encourage your readers to check them out!

Books

Bodkins, Odds. *The Christmas Cobwebs.* New York: Harcourt Brace, 2001.

Frost, Helen. *German Immigrants, 1820–1920.* Mankato, Minn.: Blue Earth Books, 2001.

Galicich, Anne. *The German Americans.* New York: Chelsea House Publishers, 1996.

Jaspersohn, William. *The Two Brothers.* Middlebury, Vt.: Vermont Folklife Center, 2000.

Nickles, Greg. *The Germans.* New York: Crabtree Publishers, 2001.

Places to Visit or Contact

German American Club
P.O. Box 1732
Lawton, OK 73502

The German American Cultural Center
519 Huey P. Long Avenue
Gretna, LA 70053

German American National Congress (DANK)
4740 North Western Avenue
Chicago, IL 60625-2097

German Pioneer Museum
4790 West Fork Road
Cincinnati, OH 45247
513-598-5732

Index